Table of Contents

It's a Girl,
page 16

*Chasing Rainbows
Table Runner,*
page 37

*Spinning Flower
Table Mat,*
page 44

Introduction

Charms are all the rage. It's hard to resist those little bundles of inspiration. Everyone wants them, everyone buys them and many question what to do with them. Charms are by far the most popular of the precut fabrics. It's a great way to get a little piece of each fabric in an entire collection. These delightful little bits of fabric can turn into beautiful quilted projects with the right instructions.

Put Some Charm in Your Quilts has nine fabulous projects to inspire you with options for paper-piecing—for those of you who have wanted to try this technique—or traditional piecing. Either way, the patterns are perfectly delightful.

Many of these lovely projects can be done with only a charm pack or less. And, for those who prefer scrappy, All Squared Up is a project that will use up all of your leftover charms or clean out the stash of charms you didn't know what to do with. You will be amazed at all you can make with charms. ■

Meet the Designer

After working as a special education teacher and raising two children, Connie Kauffman found her love of fabric, sewing, color and design; leading her to a career as a quilt designer, author and teacher.

Connie's first book, *Piecefully Amish*, was published in 2001 by the American Quilting Society. *Put Some Charm in Your Quilts* is her fifth single-author publication and her quilt designs have appeared in more than 20 hardcover books by House of White Birches. Individual patterns by Connie have been featured in *Quilter's World* magazine and *Quick & Easy Quilting*. Her designs are bright, fun and full of whimsy. ■

General Instructions

Charming aren't they—those cute little packages of 5" squares of fabric labeled as charm squares. It's hard to resist those little bundles of new fabric lines in a rainbow of colors and designs. But what do you do with them once you take them home? This book helps solve that problem with a series of paper-piecing projects ideal for using charm squares.

When paper piecing, you often need a variety of fabrics in small sizes. With a package of charms at your side, you won't have the mess of rummaging through all your fabrics to pull out coordinating bits and pieces—and charm squares are small to start with!

Purchasing Charm Square Packs

Selecting charm packs can be a fun challenge. It is tempting to buy any bundle that first takes your fancy, but here are a couple of things to consider before purchasing.

Charm packs come in a wide range of package sizes, anywhere from 20 to 50 pieces. The larger packs include repeats. Select a charm pack for your project with the appropriate colors. Look carefully at the label for the number of pieces in the package and buy more than one pack if needed. Each project in the book indicates the total number of charms needed not the number of charm packs.

Be aware that there may be a square or two in a charm package that just doesn't seem to work with your project. The color may be off, or it might be striped when you don't want a stripe. So it is helpful

to buy a few more charms than listed for your project. Don't hesitate to purchase a larger pack! The last project in this book was designed to use leftover charms and scraps—just in case you really succumb to charm squares!

Stay away from large print charm squares unless the paper-piecing block sections are large. These fabrics are lovely but not always appropriate for smaller paper-pieced projects where only portions of the fabric's design and color will be visible. In this book, Designer Notes will indicate which projects are large print friendly.

Many projects need fabric yardage for sashing, setting blocks and borders: so before purchasing charm packs, check to see if you are able to purchase coordinating yardage.

House of White Birches, Berne, Indiana 46711   Clotilde.com

4

Using this Book

The five paper-piecing blocks shown in Figure 1 are used throughout this book. Each block is used in a small project that is quick and easy and a larger project that requires more time. The Chasing Rainbows Table Runner project also includes four more paper-piecing patterns.

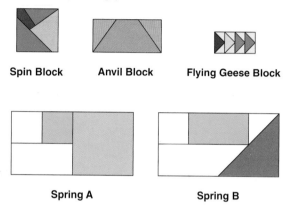

Spin Block   Anvil Block   Flying Geese Block

Spring A   Spring B

Figure 1

Patterns include paper-piecing instructions and an alternate piecing option for those of you who do not wish to try paper piecing. Alternate piecing instructions may be strip piecing or template piecing but will create the same look as the paper-piecing options. Patterns will refer to the Alternate Template Piecing general instructions when using template piecing technique. Refer to your favorite quilting guide for tips on any other quilting techniques.

The total number of charm squares needed, not the number of charm packages to purchase, are listed for each pattern. Material lists also include everything needed for either piecing option. Purchase only what is indicated for the piecing option you will be using.

Each pattern has a paper-piecing charm square Cutting Diagram that shows how to cut the charm squares into perfect usable pieces for paper-piecing each block. Many times you will be able to stack your charms and cut them together saving a lot of time.

The last project in this book, All Squared Up, is a bonus quilt that uses leftover charm squares and scraps from previous projects. Any prints will work with this bonus scrap quilt and it is a great way to use leftovers.

CutRite™ Charm Maker

The CutRite™ Charm Maker is an acrylic ruler that is great for making your own 5" charm squares from scraps and leftover yardage. It also has markings to cut the squares in half and make 2½" x 5" rectangles that can be cut again to make 2½" squares. Because the template size is exactly 5" square and there is only the one marking line on the template, it is a very easy and accurate product to use and you won't make the mistake of cutting on the wrong lines as you might with a regular ruler.

This ruler is handy to use in cutting squares from strips in All Squared Up and for cutting rectangles and squares in Spring Fling Table Mat, It's A Girl, Anvil Place Mats and Jack-in-the-Box. You can also create your own charms from leftover fabric pieces.

Paper-Piecing General Instructions

One of the oldest quilting techniques, paper piecing allows a quilter to make blocks with odd-shaped and/or small pieces. With paper piecing you can also achieve crisper points than can often be accomplished with other piecing options.

Below are general instructions for paper piecing that will be referred to in the individual patterns. It is a simple technique that can broaden the scope of a quilter's design choices.

Preparing Paper-Piecing Patterns

1. Count the paper-pieced blocks needed for your design and make that many photocopies of the block being made. There are several choices in regular papers as well as water-soluble papers that can be used. Check out choices currently available listed here and then visit your local office supply, quilt shop or online store.

Tips & Techniques

You can use many types of paper for paper-piecing patterns. Two qualities are required. You must be able to see through the paper and it must be easy to remove.

Many quilters find that ordinary copy paper is a good low cost choice. Your local office supply can also provide tracing paper, tissue paper or vellum. Copy paper and vellum can be used in printers.

Your local fabric store will offer transparent quilt block foundation paper sheets that will work in printers as well as with a wide variety of marking pens.

And for those who have problems removing any kind of paper, there is a wash-away foundation paper that can be used in printers, and with pens, pencils and rubber stamps. It will dissolve in water in about 10 seconds.

2. After printing your initial pattern, double-check to make sure it is the same size as the original pattern. Some copiers may cause slight distortion, so be sure to double-check before making all of your copies.

Tips & Techniques

When using a copy machine or printing from a computer image of your paper-piecing pattern, it is important to copy/print exactly. Even a small difference in size will make a huge difference in the overall size of your completed project.

When copying, set the copy machine to 100 percent and make a test copy. Compare the test to the original paper-piecing pattern. Your local copy store should be able to help you if you are having problems getting an exact copy.

Copy/scan/printer machines have options for printing size. Be sure to choose the "no scaling" option and a paper size to match the pattern. This should ensure an exact printed copy.

If the machine you have available is not giving you an exact copy, you will need to individually trace the number of paper-piecing patterns required for your project.

3. Cut out the patterns, leaving a margin around the outside bold lines (Figure 2). Pattern color choices can be written in each numbered space on the marked side of each pattern. All patterns are reversed on the paper copies.

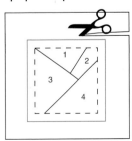

Figure 2

House of White Birches, Berne, Indiana 46711   Clotilde.com

Piecing the Blocks

1. With the printed side of the pattern facing you, fold along each line of the pattern (Figure 3), creasing the stitching lines. This will help in trimming the fabric seam allowances and in removing the paper when finished stitching.

Figure 3

2. Turn the paper pattern over with the unmarked side facing you and position fabric 1 right side up over the space marked 1. *Note: Fabric pieces for each area have been precut to cover the area and labeled with alphas in these patterns. You can also use strips or scraps that cover the area.* Hold the paper up to a light and make sure that the fabric overlaps all sides at least ¼". Pin or use a light touch of glue stick to hold in place.

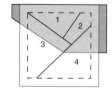

Figure 4

3. Turn the paper over with the lines facing you, and then fold the paper along the lines between sections 1 and 2. Trim fabric to about ¼" from the folded edge (Figure 5).

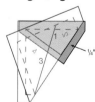

Figure 5

Figure 6

4. Place fabric piece 2 right sides together with piece 1. The edge of fabric 2 should be even with the just-trimmed edge of fabric 1 (Figure 6). Double check to see if the fabric piece chosen will cover space 2 completely by folding fabric over along line between space 1 and 2.

5. With the marked lines of paper facing you and holding fabric pieces together, place on sewing machine. Sew along the line between spaces 1 and 2 as shown in Figure 7 and use a very small stitch length (18 to 20 stitches per inch). *Note: Using a smaller stitch length will make removing paper easier because it creates a tear line at the seam.* Always begin and end sewing two to three stitches beyond the line. You do not need to backstitch. When the beginning of the stitching is at the edge of the pattern, start sewing at the solid outside line of the pattern.

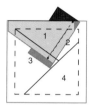

Figure 7

6. Turn pattern over, flip fabric 2 back and finger-press as shown in Figure 8.

Figure 8

7. Turn pattern over with lines facing you and fold paper away from fabric between lines 1 and 3. If there are any stitching lines extending into the fold line, slightly tear paper away from end of stitching. Trim seam allowance to ¼" (Figure 9).

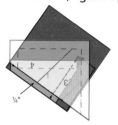

Figure 9

8. Place fabric piece 3 right sides together, even with just-trimmed edge. Turn pattern over and sew on the line between 1 and 3 (Figure 10). Turn over, flip the fabric back and finger-press (Figure 11).

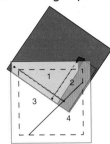

Figure 10

Figure 11

9. Continue trimming and sewing pieces in numerical order until the pattern is complete. Make sure pieces along the outer edge extend past the solid line to allow for a ¼" seam allowance (Figure 12).

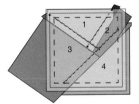

Figure 12

10. When the whole block is sewn, press the block and trim all excess fabric from the block along the outside edge solid line of paper pattern (Figure 13).

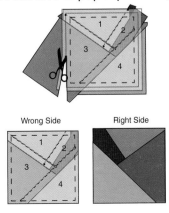

Wrong Side   Right Side

Figure 13

11. Carefully remove backing paper from completed block when indicated in pattern instructions and press seams.

12. To sew blocks or block sections together, place right sides together and carefully match edges and any matching points. Sew along the seam line still using a small stitch length if paper has not been removed yet.

Alternate Template Piecing

Some of the patterns will use templates as an alternative to paper piecing.

Prepare a template by tracing the template pattern provided onto a plastic template medium. Transfer all pattern markings and matching points. The template patterns provided include a ¼" seam allowance and a grain line.

Position the template on the wrong side of the fabric, matching the grain line to a straight grain of the fabric, and trace. Transfer all matching points to the fabric. Cut out the pattern pieces on the traced lines. ■

Spring Fling Table Mat

Ten charms and a background fabric are all you need to make your table say "spring!" Put a little charm into your next dinner.

Project Specifications
Skill Level: Beginner
Table Mat Size: 16" x 16"
Block Size: 8" x 8"
Number of Blocks: 4

Designer Note
The larger pieces in these paper-pieced sections mean you can use large print fabrics in this project even though the overall project is small.

Materials
- 10 charm squares (large or small coordinating or contrasting prints)
- ⅝ yard coordinating solid or tonal
- 1½ yards ¾"–1" wide lace trim
- Batting 18" x 18"
- 8 sheets 8½" x 11" paper (for paper piecing only)
- Fabric glue stick (for paper piecing only—optional)
- Neutral-color all-purpose thread
- Template material (for alternative piecing only)
- Quilting thread
- Basic sewing tools and supplies

Cutting
1. Choose two contrasting charms to make center squares. Referring to Cutting Diagram A, cut each charm square on one diagonal to make four pieces.

Cutting Diagram A

2. Cut four different charm squares in half, making two 2½" x 5" rectangles from each charm square, referring to Cutting Diagram B. Subcut one of the rectangles into two 2½" squares. Keep rectangle and squares from each charm square together.

Cutting Diagram B

3. Cut one 18" by fabric width strip coordinating solid or tonal; subcut one 18" square for backing and three 2½" x 24" strips for paper-piecing.

Paper-Piecing Instructions
Completing the Table Mat Top

Spring Block
8" x 8" Block
Make 4

1. Make four copies of the Spring A and B paper-piecing patterns, referring to the General Instructions on page 5 for paper and copying choices.

2. Complete the paper piecing in numerical/color order as indicated on the pattern and following the General Instructions on page 6 using similar-sized fabric shapes.

3. Sort the Spring A and Spring B completed sections into four groups of one section each as shown in Figure 1. *Note: The sample was made with a small square in Spring A section and the rectangle in Spring B section in similar colors.*

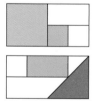

Figure 1

4. Join a Spring A and B section along a long side, referring to the block diagram, and matching seams where necessary to make a Spring block. Repeat to make four Spring blocks.

5. Join two Spring blocks with different triangles in the B sections together as seen in Figure 2 to make a row. Repeat to join the remaining two Spring blocks.

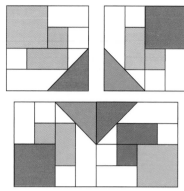

Figure 2

6. Join the rows with triangles in the center, again referring to Figure 2.

7. Remove the paper from the sections and press.

8. Mark a diagonal line on all four corners of the pieced table mat top as shown in Figure 3. Then trim the corners of the pieced table mat top, cutting on the marked diagonal lines, again referring to Figure 3.

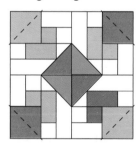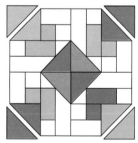

Figure 3

Completing the Table Mat

1. Position and pin the lace trim to the pieced top (Figure 4). Match the bound edge of the lace trim to the pieced top's raw edges and overlap the lace trim ends. Baste ⅛" from the edge.

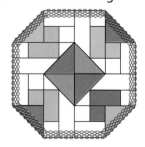

Figure 4

2. Layer backing right side up on the batting with pieced top right side down on the backing.

3. Stitch ¼" around the outside edge through all thicknesses, leaving a 3" opening on one side (Figure 5).

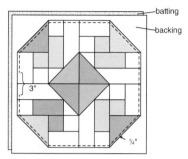

Figure 5

4. Trim backing and batting even with pieced top (Figure 6). Trim corners and then trim batting close to stitching (Figure 7).

Figure 6

Figure 7

5. Turn table mat right side out through opening. Gently push out corners with a point turner or pen. Turn seam allowances of opening to inside and hand-stitch closed.

6. Pull lace trim away from seam and press table mat flat. Quilt as desired to complete.

Alternative Piecing Instructions

Designer Note

The following instructions use the same materials listed for the paper-piecing instructions above. However, cutting and construction instructions are different. Project specifications are the same.

Spring Block
8" x 8" Block
Make 4

Cutting

1. Mark a diagonal line on each of two contrasting charm squares. Cut on the marked line to make four H triangles for block center.

2. Choose four D charm squares. ***Note:*** *The sample uses four contrasting D charm squares. These will be the corners of the table mat as seen in the Placement Diagram on page 12.*

3. Cut one 2½" x 5" E rectangle and two 2½" B squares from each of the remaining four charm squares. Lay aside 16 B squares for another project.

4. Cut one 18" by fabric width strip coordinating solid or tonal. Subcut one 18" square for backing and one 2⅞" x 22" strip and three 2½" x 22" strips from the remainder.

5. From the 2⅞" x 22" strip, cut two 2⅞" squares. Mark a diagonal line on each and cut on the line to make four F triangles.

6. From the three 2½" x 22" strips, cut eight 2½" A squares and four 2½" x 4½" C rectangles.

7. Prepare a template for G referring to page 13 in General Instructions. Use template G to cut four G rectangle shapes from the remaining strip of coordinating solid or tonal.

Completing the Spring Fling Blocks

1. Choose two A; one each C, D, F, G and H; and one each same fabric B and E.

2. Join a B and A together (Figure 1a); press seam toward A.

Figure 1a

3. Join long side of C to A-B (Figure 2a); press seam toward C.

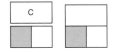

Figure 2a

4. Join D to A-B-C as shown in Figure 3a. Press seam toward D to make Section A (Figure 3a).

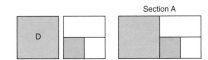

Figure 3a

5. Join A to E to F as shown in Figure 4a; press seams toward E.

Figure 4a

6. Join G to bottom of A-E-F referring to Figure 5a; press seam toward G.

Figure 5a

7. Join H to angled end of A-E-F-D as seen in Figure 6a. Press seam toward H to complete Section B.

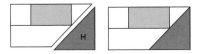

Figure 6a

8. Referring to Figure 7a and the block diagram, join Sections A and B together along long edges, matching seams where needed. Press seam toward Section A to complete a Spring Fling block.

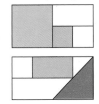

Figure 7a

9. Repeat steps 1–8 to make four Spring Fling blocks.

10. Join two blocks with different triangles in the B sections together as seen in Figure 8a to make a row. Repeat to join the remaining two blocks.

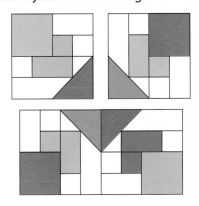

Figure 8a

House of White Birches, Berne, Indiana 46711   Clotilde.com

Completing the Table Mat

1. Join the rows with triangles in the center, again referring to Figure 8a.

2. Mark a diagonal line on all four corners of the pieced table mat top as shown in Figure 9a. Then trim the corners of the pieced table mat top, cutting on the marked diagonal lines, again referring to Figure 9a.

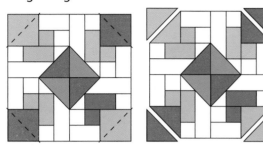

Figure 9a

3. Position and pin the lace trim to the pieced top (Figure 10a). Match the bound edge of the lace trim to the pieced top's raw edges and overlap the lace trim ends. Baste ⅛" from the edge.

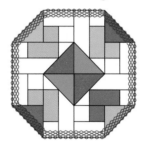

Figure 10a

4. Layer backing right side up on the batting with pieced top right side down on the backing.

5. Stitch ¼" around the outside edge through all thicknesses, leaving a 3" opening on one side (Figure 11a).

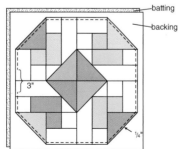

batting
backing
3"
¼"

Figure 11a

6. Trim backing and batting even with pieced top (Figure 12a). Trim corners and then trim batting close to stitching (Figure 13a).

Figure 12a

Figure 13a

7. Turn table mat right side out through opening. Gently push out corners. Turn seam allowances of opening to inside and hand-stitch closed.

8. Pull lace trim away from seam and press table mat flat. Quilt as desired to complete. ◼

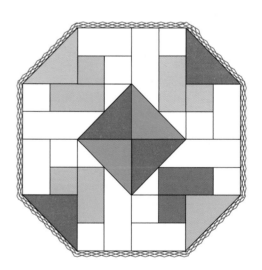

Spring Fling Table Mat
Placement Diagram 16" x 16"

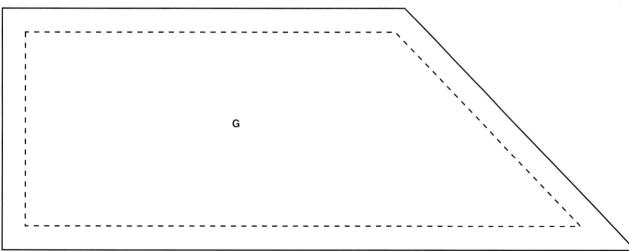

G

House of White Birches, Berne, Indiana 46711   Clotilde.com

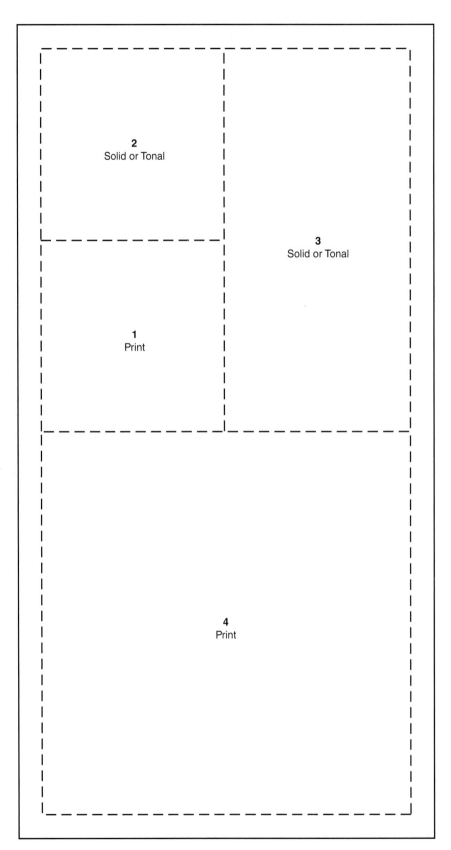

Spring A/It's a Girl A Paper-Piecing Pattern

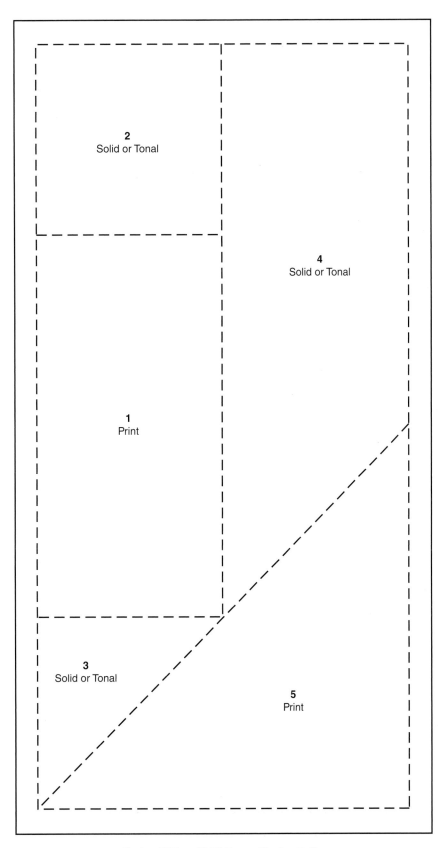

Spring B/It's a Girl B Paper-Piecing Pattern

House of White Birches, Berne, Indiana 46711   Clotilde.com

It's a Girl

Make a charming baby quilt for the next arrival. It can easily be changed to a boy theme with your choice of charms and fabrics.

Project Specifications
Skill Level: Beginner
Quilt Size: 40" x 40"
Block Size: 8" x 8"
Number of Blocks: 16

Designer Notes
The larger pieces in these paper-pieced sections mean you can use large print fabrics in this project. Choose a charm pack that has at least 36 coordinating charm squares. Eliminate any squares that do not blend well, for example black and white prints if using pastels.

Materials
- 36 coordinating charm squares
- ⅝ yard white-with-pink-dots
- 1⅛ yards coordinating blue
- Backing 48" x 48"
- Batting 48" x 48"
- Neutral-color all-purpose thread
- Quilting thread
- 16 sheets 8½" x 11" paper (for paper piecing only)
- Fabric glue stick (for paper piecing only—optional)
- Template material (for alternative piecing only)
- Basic sewing tools and supplies

Cutting
1. Trim 20 charm squares to 4½" square; set aside four different squares for A.

2. Refer to Cutting Diagram to cut 16 charm squares in half, making two 2½" x 5" rectangles from each charm square. Subcut one of the rectangles into two 2½" squares. Keep rectangle and squares from each charm square together.

Cutting Diagram

3. Cut seven 2½" by fabric width strips white-with-pink-dots. Subcut (32) 2½" squares, (16) 2½" x 4½" rectangles and (16) 2½" x 7" rectangles.

4. Cut four 4½" by fabric width coordinating blue strips; subcut into four 4½" x 32" B borders.

5. Cut one 5" by fabric width coordinating blue strip; subcut into eight 5" squares. Mark one diagonal on wrong side of each and cut to make 16 triangles for paper-piecing.

6. Cut five 2½" by fabric width coordinating blue strips for binding.

Paper-Piecing Instructions
Completing the It's a Girl Blocks

It's a Girl Block
8" x 8" Block
Make 16

1. Make 16 copies each of Spring A and B Paper-Piecing Patterns, referring to the General Instructions on page 5 for paper and copying choices.

2. Complete the paper piecing in numerical/color order as indicated on the pattern and following the General Instructions on page 6 using similar-sized fabric shapes. ***Note:*** *Use coordinating blue triangles in area 5 of the It's a Girl Paper-Piecing Pattern.*

3. Sort the It's a Girl A and B completed sections into 16 groups of one section each as shown in Figure 1.

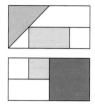

Figure 1

4. Join an It's a Girl A and B section along a long side, referring again to Figure 1 and the block diagram, and matching seams where necessary to make an It's a Girl block. Repeat to make 16 It's a Girl blocks.

5. Matching squares, join two It's a Girl blocks to make a row. Repeat to make a second row. Join the rows to make a block section with squares in the center as shown in Figure 2. Repeat to make four block sections of four blocks each, again referring to Figure 2.

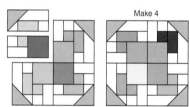

Make 4

Figure 2

6. Sew block sections together referring to the Placement Diagram on page 20 to complete the pieced center.

7. Sew a J border on opposite sides of the pieced center; press seams toward J.

8. Join I squares to either end of the remaining J borders; press seams toward J (Figure 3). Sew I/J border strips to the top and bottom of the pieced center referring to the Placement Diagram. Press seams toward I/J.

Figure 3

9. Carefully remove paper from pieced center and press.

Completing the Quilt
1. Press quilt top on both sides; check for proper seam pressing and trim all loose threads.

2. Sandwich batting between the stitched top and the prepared backing piece; pin or baste layers together to hold. Mark quilting design and quilt as desired by hand or machine.

3. When quilting is complete, remove pins or basting. Trim batting and backing fabric edges even with raw edges of quilt top.

4. Join binding strips on short ends with diagonal seams to make one long strip; trim seams to ¼" and press seams open.

5. Fold the binding strip in half with wrong sides together along length; press.

6. Sew binding to quilt edges, matching raw edges, mitering corners and overlapping ends.

7. Fold binding to the back side and stitch in place to finish.

Alternative Piecing Instructions
Designer Note
The following cutting and construction instructions are for piecing It's A Girl without paper-piecing patterns. For materials, refer to list above. This version is a Confident Beginner skill level.

It's a Girl Block
8" x 8" Block
Make 16

Cutting
1. Trim 20 charm squares to 4½" squares; set aside four different squares for I and 16 coordinating squares for D.

2. Cut one 2½" x 5" E rectangle and two 2½" B squares from each of 16 charm squares. Lay aside 16 B squares for another project.

3. Cut seven 2½" by fabric width strips white-with-pink-dots. Subcut six strips into (32) 2½" A squares, and (16) 2½" x 4½" C rectangles.

4. Prepare a template for G referring to page 5 in General Instructions. Use template G to cut 16 G rectangle shapes from the remaining white-with-pink dots strip.

5. Cut one 2⅞" by fabric width strip white-with-pink-dots; subcut eight 2⅞" F squares. Mark one diagonal line on the wrong side of each F and cut on the diagonal to make 16 F triangles.

6. Cut four 4½" by fabric width coordinating blue; subcut into four 4½" x 32" J borders.

7. Cut one 4⅞" by fabric width coordinating blue strip; subcut into eight 4⅞" H squares. Mark one diagonal on wrong side of each and cut to make 16 H triangles.

8. Cut five 2½" by fabric width coordinating blue strips for binding.

Completing the It's a Girl Blocks

1. Choose two A; one each C, D, F, G and H; and one each same fabric B and E.

2. Join a B and A together (Figure 1a); press seam toward A.

Figure 1a

3. Join long side of C to A-B (Figure 2a); press seam toward C.

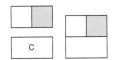

Figure 2a

4. Join D to A-B-C as shown in Figure 3a. Press seam toward D to make Section A (Figure 3a).

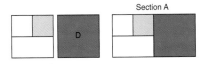

Figure 3a

5. Join A to E to F as shown in Figure 4a; press seams toward E.

Figure 4a

6. Join G to bottom of A-E-F referring to Figure 5a; press seam toward G.

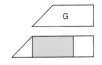

Figure 5a

7. Join H to angled end of A-E-F-D as seen in Figure 6a. Press seam toward H to complete Section B.

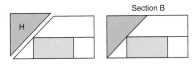

Figure 6a

8. Referring to Figure 7a and the block diagram, join Sections A and B together along long edges, matching seams where needed. Press seam toward Section A to complete an It's a Girl block.

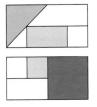

Figure 7a

9. Repeat steps 1–8 to make 16 It's a Girl blocks.

10. Matching D squares, join two It's a Girl blocks to make a row. Repeat to make a second row. Join the rows to make a block section with squares in the center as shown in Figure 8a. Repeat to make four block sections of four blocks each, again referring to Figure 8a.

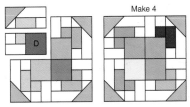

Figure 8a

11. Sew block sections together with H triangles making a center square referring to the Placement Diagram to complete the pieced center.

12. Sew a J border on opposite sides of the pieced center; press seams toward J.

13. Join I squares to either end of the remaining J borders; press seams toward J (Figure 9a). Sew I/J border strips to the top and bottom of the pieced center referring to Placement Diagram. Press seams toward I/J.

Figure 9a

House of White Birches, Berne, Indiana 46711 Clotilde.com

Completing the Quilt

1. Press quilt top on both sides; check for proper seam pressing and trim all loose threads.

2. Sandwich batting between the stitched top and the prepared backing piece; pin or baste layers together to hold. Mark quilting design and quilt as desired by hand or machine.

3. When quilting is complete, remove pins or basting. Trim batting and backing fabric edges even with raw edges of quilt top.

4. Join binding strips on short ends with diagonal seams to make one long strip; trim seams to ¼" and press seams open.

5. Fold the binding strip in half with wrong sides together along length; press.

6. Sew binding to quilt edges, matching raw edges, mitering corners and overlapping ends.

7. Fold binding to the back side and stitch in place to finish. ■

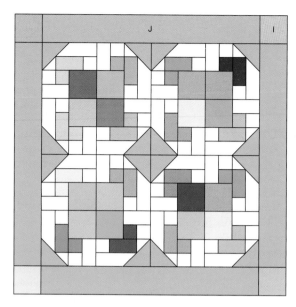

It's a Girl
Placement Diagram 40" x 40"

Anvil Place Mat

This project is a great way to use charms to add ambience to your table. The fabric you select will determine if the mats are contemporary or more traditional. There are a lot of options with this project.

Project Specifications
Skill Level: Beginner
Place Mat Size: 18½" x 12½"
Block Size: 4½" x 2"
Number of Blocks: 10

Designer Note
The materials listed make two place mats. Select a mix of 12 dark batik charm squares that will stand out against a light batik background to make two place mats. If you want the place mats to match, select six sets of two matching charm squares.

Materials
- 12 dark-color batik charm squares, variety
- ⅛ yard dark brown batik
- 1 yard coordinating light-color batik
- Batting: 2 pieces, 17" x 22" each
- Coordinating all-purpose thread
- Quilting thread
- 10 sheets 8½" x 11" paper (paper piecing only)
- Fabric glue stick (paper piecing only—optional)
- Basic sewing tools and supplies

Cutting
1. Set aside two charm squares for A. Cut the remaining 10 charm squares in half referring to the Cutting Diagram and making (20) 2½" x 5" paper-piecing shapes.

Cutting Diagram

2. Cut two 1½" by fabric width strips dark brown batik; subcut four 1½" x 13" D strips.

3. Cut one 17" by fabric width strip coordinating light-color batik; subcut two 17" x 22" rectangles for place mat backs.

4. Cut two 4½" by fabric width strips coordinating light-color batik; subcut eight 4½" B squares and eight 2½" x 4½" C rectangles.

5. Cut two 2½" by fabric width strips coordinating light-color batik; subcut (40) 2" x 2½" rectangles for paper-piecing.

Paper-Piecing Instructions

Constructing the Anvil Blocks
1. Make 20 copies of the Anvil Block Paper-Piecing Pattern, referring to the General Instructions on page 5 for paper and copying choices.

2. Complete the paper piecing in numerical/color order as indicated on the pattern and following the General Instructions on page 6 using similar-sized fabric shapes and referring to Figure 1.

Anvil Block
Make 20

Figure 1

Piecing the Place Mat Tops
1. Join a C rectangle to both short ends of an Anvil block as seen in Figure 2 to make a side row; press seams toward C. Repeat to make four side rows.

Side Row
Make 4

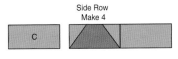

Figure 2

House of White Birches, Berne, Indiana 46711 Clotilde.com

2. Join two Anvil blocks together along their top and bottom edges as shown in Figure 3; press seam toward wide end of triangular shape in Anvil block. Repeat to make eight Anvil sections.

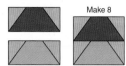

Make 8

Figure 3

3. Join B on both sides of an Anvil section as shown in Figure 4; press seams toward B. Repeat to make four top/bottom rows.

Top/Bottom Row
Make 4

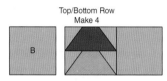

Figure 4

4. Join an Anvil section on opposite sides of A to make a center row (Figure 5). Press seams toward A. Repeat to make two center rows.

Center Row
Make 2

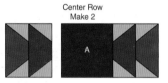

Figure 5

5. Sew a top/bottom row on both long sides of a center row to make the pieced center of the place mat referring to Figure 6. Press seams in one direction.

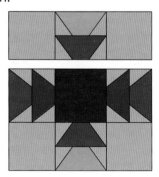

Figure 6

6. Referring to Figure 7 for orientation, sew a D strip and side row to opposite sides of the pieced center. Press seams toward D to complete a place mat top.

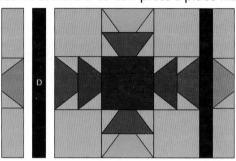

Figure 7

7. Repeat steps 4–6 to complete a second place mat top.

8. Carefully remove the paper from the paper-piecing sections of each place mat top and press.

Completing the Place Mats

1. Layer together the batting with backing faceup and quilt top facedown.

2. Sew ¼" around the outside edges, leaving a 3" opening on one side for turning.

3. Trim corners; then trim batting close to the stitching. Turn inside out through opening, pushing corners out.

4. Turn opening seam allowance to inside and hand-stitch closed.

5. Press and quilt as desired.

Alternative Piecing Instructions

Designer Note
Project specifications and materials listed for the paper-piecing instructions are the same for the following alternative instructions. The cutting and construction instructions below should be followed if you do not wish to use the paper-piecing technique.

Anvil
2" x 4½" Block
Make 20

Cutting

1. Set aside two charm squares for A. Cut (20) 2½" x 5" F rectangles from the remaining 10 charm squares.

2. Cut two 1½" by fabric width strips dark brown batik; subcut four 1½" x 13" D strips.

3. Cut one 17" by fabric width strip coordinating light-color batik; subcut two 17" x 22" rectangles for place mat backs.

4. Cut two 4½" by fabric width strips coordinating light-color batik; subcut eight 4½" B squares and eight 2½" x 4½" C rectangles.

5. Cut two 2½" by fabric width strips coordinating light-color batik; subcut (40) 2" x 2½" E rectangles.

Constructing the Anvil Blocks

1. Mark a diagonal line on the wrong side of each E rectangle (Figure 1a).

Figure 1a

2. Position E on F, matching the 2½" sides referring to Figure 2a. Stitch along the marked line. Trim the seam allowance to ¼" and press E away from F, again referring to Figure 2a.

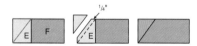

Figure 2a

3. Repeat step 2 on the opposite end of F referring to Figure 3a. Repeat to make 20 Anvil units.

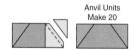

Figure 3a

Piecing the Place Mat Tops

1. Join a C rectangle to both short ends of an Anvil unit as shown in Figure 4a to make a side row; press seams toward C. Repeat to make four side rows.

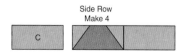

Figure 4a

2. Join two Anvil units together along their top and bottom edges as shown in Figure 5a; press seam toward wide end of triangular shape in Anvil unit. Repeat to make eight Anvil sections.

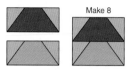

Figure 5a

3. Join B on both sides of an Anvil section as shown in Figure 6a; press seams toward B. Repeat to make four top/bottom rows.

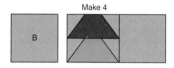

Figure 6a

4. Join an Anvil section on opposite sides of A to make a center row (Figure 7a). Press seams toward A. Repeat to make two center rows.

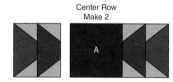

Figure 7a

5. Sew a top/bottom row on both long sides of a center row to make the pieced center of the place mat referring to Figure 8a. Press seams in one direction.

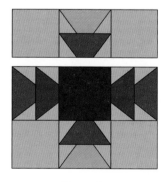

Figure 8a

6. Referring to Figure 9a for orientation, sew a D strip and side row to opposite sides of the pieced center. Press seams toward D to complete a place mat top.

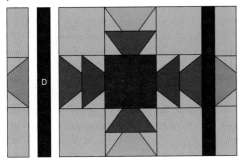

Figure 9a

7. Repeat steps 5 and 6 to complete a second place mat top.

Completing the Place Mats

1. Layer the batting with backing faceup and quilt top facedown.

2. Sew ¼" seam around the outside edges, leaving a 3" opening on one side for turning.

3. Trim corners and seam allowances. Then, trim batting close to the stitching. Turn right side out through opening, gently pushing corners out.

4. Turn opening seam allowance to inside and hand-stitch closed.

5. Press and quilt as desired. ■

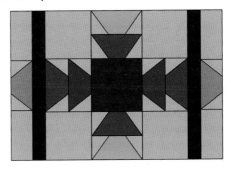

Anvil Place Mats
Placement Diagram 18½" x 12½"

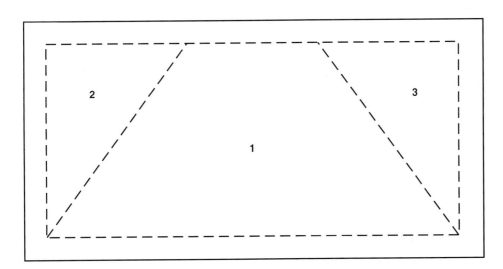

Anvil Block Paper-Piecing Pattern
For Anvil Place Mats: Use Dark Batik for 1 and Light Batik for 2 and 3
For Jack-in-the-Box quilt: Use Primary Color for 1 and White Tone-on-Tone for 2 and 3

Jack-in-the-Box

Cheer up any room with this one-of-a-kind treasure.
Pick your charms and determine the theme.

Project Specifications
Skill Level: Beginner
Quilt Size: 51½" x 64"
Block Size: 12½" x 12½"
Number of Blocks: 12

Designer Note
The sample quilt uses 60 charm squares in bright and cheerful primary colors. Since charm square packs vary in number of pieces, this quilt will require two or more charm packs. Twelve tone-on-tone or mini-print charms were chosen for the block centers.

Materials
• 60 primary-color charm squares
• ½ yard bright yellow print
• ⅝ yard red/pink stripe
• 1¼ yards white tone-on-tone
• 1⅔ yard bright green print
• Backing 59" x 72"
• Batting 59" x 72"
• Neutral-color all-purpose thread
• Quilting thread
• 96 sheets 8½" x 11" paper (paper piecing only)
• Fabric glue stick (paper piecing only—optional)
• Basic sewing tools and supplies

Cutting
1. Set aside 12 tone-on-tone or mini-print charm squares for A.

2. Cut 48 charm squares in half referring to the Cutting Diagram and making (96) 2½" x 5" paper-piecing shapes.

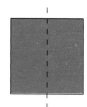

Cutting Diagram

3. Cut five 2½" by fabric width E/F strips bright yellow print.

4. Cut seven 2½" by fabric width strips red/pink stripe for binding.

5. Cut six 4½" by fabric width tone-on-tone white strips; subcut into (48) 4½" B squares.

6. Cut (10) 2½" by fabric width strips tone-on-tone white; subcut into (192) 2" x 2½" paper-piecing shapes.

7. Cut two 5½" x 54½" G border strips and two 5½" x 51½" H border strips bright green print along length.

Paper-Piecing Instructions
Constructing the Jack-in-the-Box Blocks

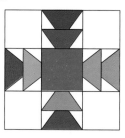

Jack-in-the-Box
12½" x 12½" Block
Make 12

1. Make 96 copies of the Anvil Block Paper-Piecing Pattern found on page 25, referring to the General Instructions on page 5 for paper and copying choices.

2. Complete the paper piecing in numerical/color order as indicated on the pattern, following the General Instructions on page 6 using similar-sized fabric shapes and referring to Figure 1.

Anvil Block
Make 10

Figure 1

3. Join two Anvil sections together along their top and bottom edges as shown in Figure 2; press seam toward wide end of triangular shape in Anvil section. Repeat to make four Anvil sections.

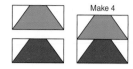

Make 4

Figure 2

4. Join a B square to both short ends of an Anvil section as seen in Figure 3 to make a side row; press seams toward B. Repeat to make two top/bottom rows.

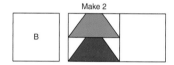

Make 2

Figure 3

5. Join an Anvil section to opposite sides of A to make a center row (Figure 4). Press seams toward A.

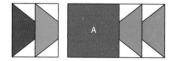

Figure 4

6. Sew a top/bottom row on opposite long sides of the center row to make a Jack-in-the-Box block referring to Figure 5. Press seams in one direction.

Figure 5

7. Repeat steps 3–7 to make 12 Jack-in-the-Box blocks.

Completing the Quilt Top

1. Arrange and stitch three Jack-in-the-Box blocks into a row, rotating the blocks so that seams are pressed in opposite directions and referring to Figure 6. Press seams in one direction.

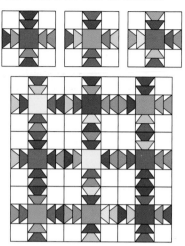

Figure 6

2. Repeat to make four rows; pressing seams in opposite directions every other row. Stitch rows together matching seams, again referring to Figure 6 to make the pieced center.

3. Join three E/F strips together on short ends; press seams to one side. Cut two 50½" E strips. Trim remaining E/F strips to 42" for F.

4. Referring to the Placement Diagram, stitch E to opposite long sides of the pieced center; press seams toward E. Stitch F to the top and bottom of the pieced center; press seams toward F

5. Carefully remove paper from Jack-in-the-Box blocks.

6. Stitch G to opposite long sides and H to top and bottom of the quilt referring to the Placement Diagram on page 31. Press seams toward G and then H.

Completing the Quilt

1. Press quilt top on both sides; check for proper seam pressing and trim all loose threads.

2. Sandwich batting between the stitched top and the prepared backing piece; pin or baste layers together to hold. Mark quilting design and quilt as desired by hand or machine.

3. When quilting is complete, remove pins or basting. Trim batting and backing fabric edges even with raw edges of quilt top.

4. Join binding strips on short ends with diagonal seams to make one long strip; trim seams to ¼" and press seams open.

5. Fold the binding strip in half with wrong sides together along length; press.

6. Sew binding to quilt edges, matching raw edges, mitering corners and overlapping ends.

7. Fold binding to the back side and stitch in place to finish.

Alternative Piecing Instructions

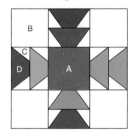

Jack-in-the-Box
12½" x 12½" Block
Make 12

Designer Note
Project specifications and materials listed for the paper-piecing instructions are the same for the following alternative instructions. The cutting and construction instructions below should be followed if you do not wish to use the paper-piecing technique.

Cutting
1. Set aside 12 tone-on-tone or mini-print charm squares for A.

2. Cut 48 charm squares in half to make (96) 2½" x 5" D rectangles.

3. Cut five 2½" by fabric width E/F strips bright yellow print.

4. Cut seven 2½" by fabric width strips red/pink stripe for binding.

5. Cut six 4½" by fabric width tone-on-tone white strips; subcut into (48) 4½" B squares.

6. Cut (10) 2½" by fabric width strips tone-on-tone white; subcut into (192) 2" x 2½" C rectangles.

7. Cut two 5½" x 54½" G border strips and two 5½" x 51½" H border strips bright green print along length.

Constructing the Anvil Blocks

1. Mark a diagonal line on the wrong side of each C rectangle (Figure 1a).

Figure 1a

2. Position C on D, matching the 2½" sides referring to Figure 2a. Stitch along the marked line. Trim the seam allowance to ¼" and press C away from D, again referring to Figure 2a.

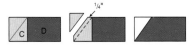

Figure 2a

3. Repeat step 2 on the opposite end of D referring to Figure 3a. Repeat to make 96 Anvil units.

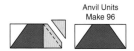

Figure 3a

4. Join two Anvil units together along their top and bottom edges as shown in Figure 4a; press seam toward wide end of triangular shape in Anvil unit. Repeat to make four Anvil sections.

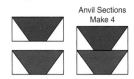

Figure 4a

5. Join B to both sides of an Anvil section as shown in Figure 5a; press seams toward B. Repeat to make two top/bottom rows.

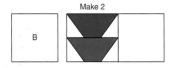

Figure 5a

6. Join an Anvil section to opposite sides of A to make a center row (Figure 6a). Press seams toward A.

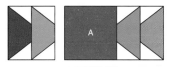

Figure 6a

7. Sew a top/bottom row on both long sides of a center row to make a Jack-in-the-Box block referring to Figure 7a. Press seams in one direction.

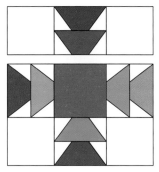

Figure 7a

8. Repeat steps 4–7 to make 12 Jack-in-the-Box blocks.

Completing the Quilt Top

1. Arrange and stitch three Jack-in-the-Box blocks into a row, rotating the blocks so that seams are pressed in opposite directions and referring to Figure 8a. Press seams in one direction.

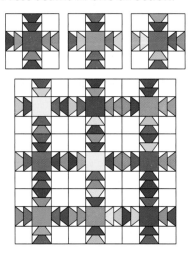

Figure 8a

2. Repeat to make four rows; pressing seams in opposite directions every other row. Stitch rows together matching seams, again referring to Figure 8a to make the pieced center.

3. Join three E/F strips together on short ends; press seams to one side. Cut two 50½" E strips. Trim remaining E/F strips to 42" for F.

4. Referring to the Placement Diagram, stitch E to opposite long sides of the pieced center; press seams toward E. Stitch F to the top and bottom of the pieced center; press seams toward F.

5. Carefully remove paper from Anvil blocks.

6. Stitch G to opposite long sides and H to top and bottom of the quilt referring to the Placement Diagram. Press seams toward G and then H.

Completing the Quilt
1. Press quilt top on both sides; check for proper seam pressing and trim all loose threads.

2. Sandwich batting between the stitched top and the prepared backing piece; pin or baste layers together to hold. Mark quilting design and quilt as desired by hand or machine.

3. When quilting is complete, remove pins or basting. Trim batting and backing fabric edges even with raw edges of quilt top.

4. Join binding strips on short ends with diagonal seams to make one long strip; trim seams to ¼" and press seams open.

5. Fold the binding strip in half with wrong sides together along length; press.

6. Sew binding to quilt edges, matching raw edges, mitering corners and overlapping ends.

7. Fold binding to the back side and stitch in place to finish. ■

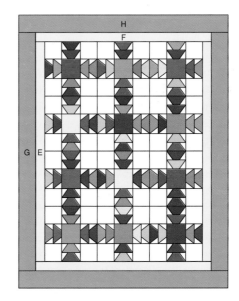

Jack-in-the-Box
51½" x 64" Placement Diagram

House of White Birches, Berne, Indiana 46711 Clotilde.com

Floral Coasters

Make a set of these lovely coasters for each of your friends. These cuties also double as a small hot pad. They are a great make-ahead gift to have on hand.

Project Specifications
Skill Level: Confident Beginner
Coaster Size: 6" x 6"

Designer Notes
This pattern gives materials and instructions for one coaster. To make more, simply increase the amounts given by the number of coasters you wish to make.

Choose a charm square for the coaster center with a large print that can be fussy-cut to create a focal design—like the flowers in the samples. Then choose two different, complementary-colored, small print charm squares for the flying geese units.

For coasters, use a thin batting that will allow a glass or cup to sit firmly without tipping! For small hot pad, use a needle-punched insulating batting.

Materials
- 3 coordinating charm squares
    1 large floral print
    1 each light and dark pink small floral print
- ¼ yard green floral print
- Batting 7" x 7"
- Coordinating-color all-purpose thread
- 4 sheets 8½" x 11" paper (paper piecing only)
- Fabric glue stick (paper piecing only—optional)
- Basic sewing tools and supplies

Cutting
1. Referring to the Cutting Diagram, cut one each light and dark pink small floral print charm square in half making two 2½" x 5" rectangles. Subcut each rectangle into four 1¼" x 2½" shapes, making eight light and eight dark pink paper-piecing shapes.

Cutting Diagram

2. Fussy-cut a 3½" A square from the large floral print charm square, centering on a single floral design if possible.

3. Cut one 7" by fabric width green floral print strip. Subcut one 7" backing square. **Note:** *To use more charm squares in this project, piece four charm squares together in a square and use as the backing for the coaster.*

4. From the remainder of the 7" green floral print strip, cut one 1½" x 35" strip. Subcut the strip into (32) 1" x 1½" paper-piecing shapes.

5. Cut two 2⅜" squares from the green floral print scraps. Mark one diagonal line on the wrong side of each square and cut on the line to make four B triangles.

Paper-Piecing Instructions

Completing the Flying Geese Units
1. Make four copies of the Flying Geese Paper-Piecing Pattern, referring to the General Instructions on page 5 for paper and copying choices.

2. Complete the paper piecing in numerical/color order as indicated on the pattern and follow the General Instructions on page 6 using similar-sized fabric shapes to make two each of two different Flying Geese units as seen in Figure 1.

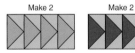

Figure 1

Piecing the Coaster Top
1. Join two light Flying Geese units to opposite sides of A as shown in Figure 2.

Figure 2

2. Join a B triangle to both ends of the dark Flying Geese unit referring to Figure 3. Repeat to make a second B-Flying Geese section.

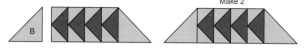

Make 2

Figure 3

3. Stitch the B-Flying Geese units to the top and bottom of the coaster (Figure 4).

Figure 4

Completing the Coaster

1. Layer the batting with the 7" backing square faceup and the coaster top facedown (Figure 5).

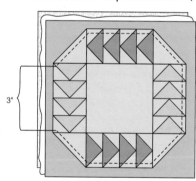

3"

Figure 5

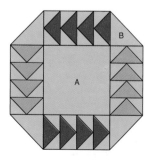

Floral Coasters
Placement Diagram 6" x 6"

2. Stitch ¼" from the outside edge all around, leaving a 3" opening for turning right side out, referring again to Figure 5.

3. Trim corners and seam allowances (Figure 6). Trim the batting close to the seam (Figure 7). Turn inside out through opening.

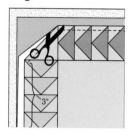

3"

Figure 6

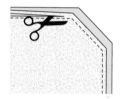

Figure 7

4. Turn opening seam allowances to inside and hand-stitch closed. Press coaster flat.

5. Quilt as desired to complete the coaster.

Alternative Piecing Instructions

Designer Note
Project specifications and materials listed for the paper-piecing instructions are the same for the following alternative instructions. The cutting and construction instructions below should be followed if you do not wish to use the paper-piecing technique.

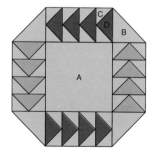

Floral Coasters
Placement Diagram 6" x 6"

Cutting
1. Cut eight 1¼" x 2" D rectangles from each light and dark charm square.

2. Fussy-cut a 3½" A square from the large floral print charm square, centering on a single floral design if possible.

3. Cut one 7" by fabric width green floral print strip. Subcut one 7" backing square. *Note: To use more charm squares in this project, piece four extra charm squares together in a square and use as the backing for the coaster.*

4. From the remainder of the 7" green floral print strip, cut one 1¼" x 35" strip. Subcut the strip into (32) 1¼" C squares.

5. Cut two 2⅜" squares from the green floral print scraps. Mark one diagonal line on the wrong side of each square and cut on the line to make four B triangles.

Piecing the Flying Geese Units

1. Mark one diagonal on the wrong side of each C square.

2. Position a C square on one end of a dark D rectangle as seen in Figure 1a and stitch on the marked diagonal line. Trim the seam allowance to ¼" and press C away from D. Repeat stitching a second C square to the opposite end of D, again referring to Figure 1a.

Figure 1a

3. Repeat step 2 to make eight dark Flying Geese
4. Using light D rectangles, repeat steps 2 and 3 to make eight light Flying Geese (Figure 2a).

Figure 2a

5. Choose four light Flying Geese and join on long sides as shown in Figure 3a with points of center triangles facing in the same direction. Repeat to make two Light Flying Geese units.

Figure 3a

6. Repeat with dark Flying Geese to make two Dark Flying Geese units as shown in Figure 3a.

7. Join two Light Flying Geese units to opposite sides of A as shown in Figure 4a.

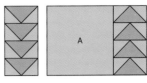

Figure 4a

8. Join a B triangle to both ends of the Dark Flying Geese unit referring to Figure 5a. Repeat to make a second B-Flying Geese section.

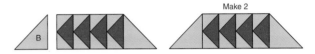

Figure 5a

9. Stitch the B-Flying Geese units to the top and bottom of the coaster (Figure 6a).

Figure 6a

Completing the Coaster

1. Layer the batting with the 7" backing square faceup and the coaster top facedown (Figure 7a).

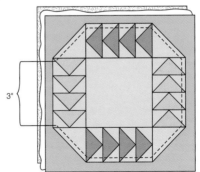

Figure 7a

2. Stitch ¼" from the outside edge all around, leaving a 3" opening for turning right side out, referring again to Figure 7a.

3. Trim corners and seam allowances (Figure 8a). Trim the batting close to the seam (Figure 9a). Turn inside out through opening.

4. Turn opening seam allowances to inside and hand-stitch closed. Press coaster flat.

5. Quilt as desired to complete the coaster. ▪

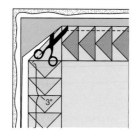

Figure 8a

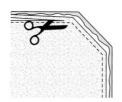

Figure 9a

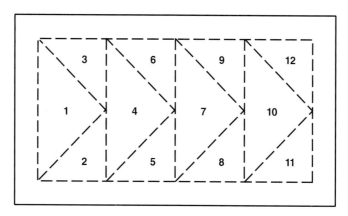

Flying Geese Paper-Piecing Pattern
Make 4 copies for Floral Coasters
Use Light or Dark Pink in 1, 4, 7 & 10
Use Green Floral in 2, 3, 5, 6, 8, 9, 11 & 12

Make 24 copies for Chasing Rainbows Table Runner
Use Bright Rainbow colors in 1, 4, 7 & 10
Use Light Cream in 2, 3, 5, 6, 8, 9, 11 & 12

Chasing Rainbows Table Runner

A great project to add some glorious color to your table with little morsels of charm squares.

Project Specifications
Skill Level: Intermediate
Quilt Size: 24" x 12"
Block Size: 3" x 3"
Number of Blocks: 10

Designer Notes
The pieces are small on this quilt, so tonal fabrics or very small prints work best. Choose a nice variety of 32 charm squares in bright, rainbow-colored fabrics.

This project uses five paper-piecing patterns instead of one: Flying Geese on page 36 and Patterns A–D on page 42.

Materials
- 32 charm squares, variety bright rainbow colors
- ⅞ yard light cream
- Batting 16" x 28"
- Neutral-color all-purpose thread
- Quilting thread
- 34 sheets 8½" x 11" paper (paper piecing only)
- Fabric glue stick (paper piecing only–optional)
- Basic sewing tools and supplies

Cutting
1. Select eight charm squares. Cut four of the charm squares into 3⅞" squares; mark one diagonal on wrong side of each, then subcut on diagonals to make eight E triangles. Set aside four triangles for another project.

2. Cut remaining four charm squares into 3½" F squares.

3. Cut 24 charm squares in half making (48) 2½" x 5" rectangles. Cut 24 of the rectangles into four

1¼" x 2½" shapes, each rectangle, making 96 paper-piecing shapes referring to the Cutting Diagram.

Cutting Diagram

4. Cut the remaining 24 rectangles into two 2½" squares each, again referring to the Cutting Diagram. Subcut 24 of the squares in half on one diagonal, making 48 triangles. Select 28 triangles for paper-piecing. Set aside remaining triangles and squares for another project.

5. Cut one 16" by fabric width light cream strip; subcut one 16" x 28" rectangle for backing. Cut remaining strip into six 1½" x 14" strips; subcut strips into (52) 1½" paper-piecing squares.

6. Cut five 1½" by fabric width light cream strips; subcut strips into (140) 1½" paper-piecing squares.

7. Cut one 2" by fabric width light cream strip; subcut strip into (21) 2" paper-piecing squares.

Paper-Piecing Instructions
Constructing the Paper-Pieced Units
1. Make 24 copies of Flying Geese, 8 copies of A and two copies each of B, C and D paper-piecing patterns referring to the General Instructions on page 5 for paper and copying choices.

2. Complete the paper piecing in numerical order as indicated on each pattern and following the

General Instructions on page 6 using similar-sized fabric shapes, mixing colors and referring to diagrams for how many of each to make.

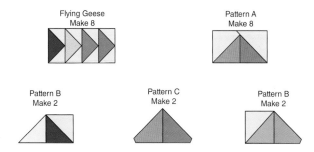

Flying Geese
Make 8

Pattern A
Make 8

Pattern B
Make 2

Pattern C
Make 2

Pattern B
Make 2

3. Set aside four Flying Geese units. From the remaining 20 units, select and join two Flying Geese units together along the long sides as seen in Figure 1 to make a Flying Geese section; press seams in one direction. Repeat to make 10 Flying Geese sections. *Note: Arrange Flying Geese units so that the same color is not side by side in the completed section.*

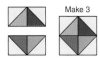

Make 10

Figure 1

4. Select two different A units and join, matching center seams (Figure 2); press seam in one direction. Repeat to make three A sections, again referring to Figure 2. *Note: Arrange A units so that the same color is not side by side in the A square.*

Make 3

Figure 2

Completing the Table Runner

1. Select one each A, B and D units and two of the Flying Geese units set aside in step 3 of Constructing the Paper-Pieced Units. Refer to Figure 3 for orientation of units and join to make row 1. Press seams in one direction. Repeat to make two rows.

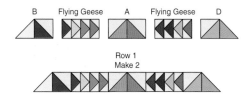

B   Flying Geese   A   Flying Geese   D

Row 1
Make 2

Figure 3

2. Select two each E and F and three Flying Geese sections. Refer to Figure 4 for orientation, paying attention to direction of the Flying Geese blocks, and join to make row 2. Press seams in one direction. Repeat to make two rows.

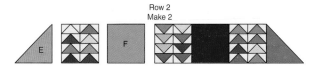

Row 2
Make 2

E   F

Figure 4

3. Select two C, three A sections and four Flying Geese sections. Refer to Figure 5 for orientation, again paying attention to direction of the Flying Geese sections, and join to make the center row. Press seams in one direction.

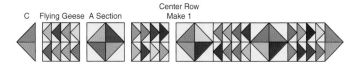

C   Flying Geese   A Section

Center Row
Make 1

Figure 5

4. Carefully remove the paper from each row. Re-press seams.

5. Referring to Figure 6, stitch rows together, matching seams and rotating rows as shown. Press seams in one direction.

Figure 6

6. Layer together the batting with backing faceup and quilt top facedown.

7. Sew ¼" around the outside edges, leaving a 3" opening on one side.

8. Trim corners; then trim batting close to the stitching. Turn right side out through the opening, pushing corners out.

9. Turn opening seam allowance to inside and hand-stitch closed.

10. Press flat and quilt as desired.

Alternative Piecing Instructions

Designer Note

Project specifications and materials listed for the paper-piecing instructions are the same for the following alternative instructions. The cutting and construction instructions below should be followed if you do not wish to use the paper-piecing technique.

Cutting

1. Select four charm squares. Cut four of the charm squares into 3⅞" squares; mark one diagonal on wrong side of each, then subcut on diagonal to make a total of eight E triangles. Set aside four triangles for another project.

2. Cut remaining four charm squares into 3½" F squares.

3. Cut one 2" x 5" strip from each of 24 charm squares. Subcut the 2" x 5" strips into four 1¼" x 2" A rectangles for a total of 96 A rectangles.

4. Cut (14) 2⅜" squares from the charm square scraps. Mark one diagonal on the wrong side of each square. Cut on the diagonal to make 28 B triangles.

5. Cut one 16" by fabric width light cream strip; subcut one 16" x 28" rectangle for backing. Cut remaining strip into two 2⅜" x 14" strips; subcut strips into (10) 2⅜" squares. Mark one diagonal on the wrong side of each square and cut on diagonal to make 20 D triangles.

6. Cut five 1¼" by fabric width light cream strips; subcut a total of (192) 1¼" C squares.

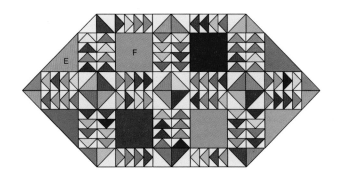

Chasing Rainbows Table Runner
Placement Diagram 24" x 12"

Constructing Pieced Units

1. Mark one diagonal on the wrong side of each C square.

2. Position a C square on one end of an A rectangle as seen in Figure 1a and stitch on the marked diagonal line. Trim the seam allowance to ¼" and press C away from A. Repeat stitching a second C square to the opposite end of A, again referring to Figure 1a.

Figure 1a

3. Repeat step 2 to make 96 Flying Geese.

4. Join four Flying Geese on long sides as shown in Figure 2a with triangles facing in the same direction. Repeat to make 24 Flying Geese sections.

Figure 2a

5. Join a D triangle to a B triangle along the angled sides as shown in Figure 3a; press seam toward F. Repeat to make 20 B/D squares.

Figure 3a

6. Join the B sides of two B/D squares together to make a B-D unit (Figure 4a). Press seam to one side. Repeat to make eight G sections; set two aside.

Figure 4a

7. Refer to Figure 5a and join two G units to make a square; press seam in one direction. Repeat to make three G squares.

Figure 5a

8. Join a B-D unit to a B triangle referring to Figure 6a for orientation; press seam toward B-D unit. Repeat to make two I sections.

Figure 6a

9. Referring to Figure 7a, reverse the B-D unit and join a B triangle to the B side of the B-D unit. Repeat to make two H sections.

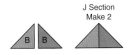

Figure 7a

10. Choose two different B triangles and join along a short side as seen in Figure 8a. Repeat to make two J sections.

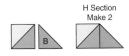

Figure 8a

Completing the Table Runner

1. Select one each G, H and I sections and two Flying Geese sections. Refer to Figure 9a for orientation of units and join to make row 1. Press seams in one direction. Repeat to make two rows.

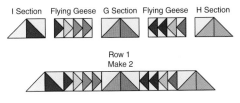

Figure 9a

2. Select two each E and F and six Flying Geese sections. Refer to Figure 10a for orientation, pay attention to the direction of the Flying Geese units and join to make row 2. Press seams in one direction. Repeat to make two rows.

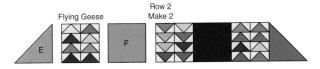

Figure 10a

3. Select two F units, three G squares and eight Flying Geese units. Refer to Figure 11a for orientation, again paying attention to the Flying Geese sections, and join to make the center row. Press seams in one direction.

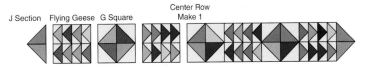

Figure 11a

4. Referring to Figure 12a, stitch rows together, matching seams. Press seams in one direction.

Figure 12a

5. Layer together the batting with backing faceup and quilt top facedown.

6. Sew ¼" around the outside edges, leaving a 3" opening on one side.

7. Trim corners; then trim batting close to the stitching. Turn right side out through the opening, pushing corners out.

8. Turn opening seam allowance to inside and hand-stitch closed.

9. Press flat and quilt as desired to complete. ■

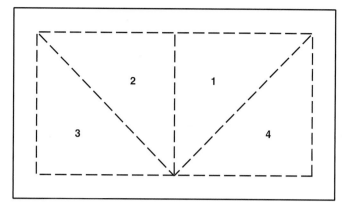

Chasing Rainbows Paper-Piecing Pattern A
Make 8 copies
Use colors in areas 1 and 2. Use light cream in areas 3 and 4.

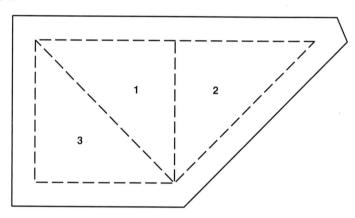

Chasing Rainbows Paper-Piecing Pattern B
Make 2 copies
Use colors in areas 1 and 2. Use light cream in area 3.

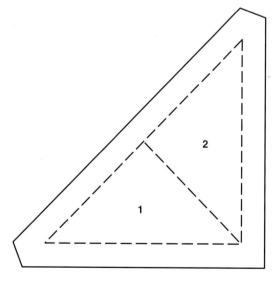

Chasing Rainbows Paper-Piecing Pattern C
Make 2 copies
Use colors in areas 1 and 2.

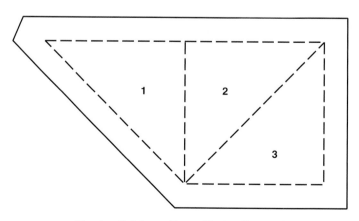

Chasing Rainbows Paper-Piecing Pattern D
Make 2 copies
Use colors in areas 2 and 3. Use light cream in area 1.

Spinning Flower Table Mat

Sixteen charms, a touch of black and a background fabric will turn your table into a conversation piece. Every table should have at least one.

Project Specifications
Skill Level: Confident Beginner
Table Mat Size: 24" x 24"
Block Size: 4½" x 4½"
Number of Blocks: 16

Designer Note
The blades of the pinwheel in this design are larger pieces that lend themselves to using large print fabrics even though the overall project is small. A mix of colors in the blades of the pinwheel gives added interest to the design.

Materials
• 16 coordinating bright charm squares
• ⅛ yard solid black
• 1 yard coordinating blue
• Backing 30" x 30"
• Batting 30" x 30"
• 16 sheets 8½" x 11" paper (paper piecing only)
• Fabric glue stick (paper piecing only—optional)
• Template material (alternate piecing only)
• 4 (¾") coordinating color buttons
• 4 (1¼") black buttons
• Neutral-color all-purpose thread
• Quilting thread
• Basic sewing tools and supplies

Cutting
No pre-cutting of the charm squares is necessary for this paper-piecing pattern.

1. Cut one 8⅞" by fabric width coordinating blue strip; subcut two 8⅞" squares. Cut each square on one diagonal to make four B triangles.

2. Cut one 8½" A square from the remaining 8⅞" coordinating blue strip.

3. Cut four 3¼" by fabric width coordinating blue strips; subcut 16 each 3¼" x 5" and 3¼" x 4" paper-piecing shapes.

4. Cut three 2½" by fabric width coordinating blue strips for binding.

5. Cut two 2" by fabric width solid black strips; subcut into (16) 2" x 4" paper-piecing shapes.

Paper-Piecing Instructions
Completing the Quilted Top
1. Make 16 copies of the Spin block Paper-Piecing Pattern, referring to the General Instructions on page 5 for paper and copying choices.

2. Complete the paper piecing in numerical order as indicated on the pattern and following the General Instructions on page 6 using similar-sized fabric shapes (Figure 1). Place coordinating blue shapes in areas 1 and 4, the solid black shape in area 2 and the charm squares in area 3, to make 16 Spin blocks

Spin Block
Make 10

Figure 1

3. Arrange the Spin blocks in sets of four, coordinating the charm square areas to create a spinning flower as shown in Figure 2.

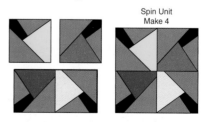

Spin Unit
Make 4

Figure 2

4. Join two of the Spin blocks into a row. Repeat to make two rows. Join the two rows to make a Spin unit as seen in Figure 2. Repeat to make four Spin units.

5. Carefully remove paper from each Spin unit and press.

6. Join a B triangle to opposite sides of a Spin unit (Figure 3). Press seams toward B. Repeat to make two top/bottom rows.

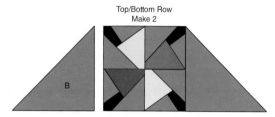

Top/Bottom Row
Make 2

Figure 3

7. Join a Spin unit to opposite sides of A to make the center row (Figure 4). Press seams toward A.

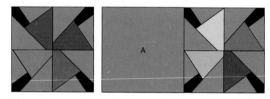

Figure 4

8. Refer to the Placement Diagram and sew a top/bottom row to either side of the center row to complete the pieced top.

Completing the Table Mat

1. Press the table mat top on both sides; check for proper seam pressing and trim all loose threads.

2. Sandwich batting between the stitched top and the prepared backing piece; pin or baste layers together to hold. Mark quilting design and quilt as desired by hand or machine.

3. When quilting is complete, remove pins or basting. Trim batting and backing fabric edges even with raw edges of quilt top.

4. Join binding strips on short ends with diagonal seams to make one long strip; trim seams to ¼" and press seams open.

5. Fold the binding strip in half with wrong sides together along length; press.

6. Sew binding to quilt edges, matching raw edges, mitering corners and overlapping ends.

7. Fold binding to the back side and stitch in place.

8. Stack a colored ¾" button on a black 1¼" button and stitch to table mat at center of Spin units referring to Placement Diagram to finish.

Alternate Piecing Instructions

Designer Note
The following instructions use the same materials listed for the paper-piecing instructions above. Project specifications are the same. However, cutting and construction instructions are different.

Spin Block
4½" x 4½"
Make 10

Cutting
1. Prepare templates C–F referring to page 7 in General Instructions.

2. Use template D to cut 16 D pieces from the charm squares.

3. Use template E to cut 16 E solid black pieces.

4. Cut one 8⅞" by fabric width coordinating blue strip; subcut two 8⅞" squares. Cut each square on one diagonal to make four B triangles.

5. Cut one 8½" A square from the remaining 8⅞" coordinating blue strip.

6. Cut three 2½" by fabric width coordinating blue strips for binding.

7. Use templates C and F to cut 16 each C and F pieces from the remaining coordinating blue fabric.

Completing the Spin Blocks
1. Refer to Figure 1a and join C to E; press seam toward E.

2. Join D to C/E as shown in Figure 2a; press seam toward D.

Figure 1a

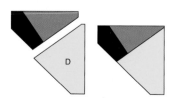

Figure 2a

3. Refer to Figure 3a and join F to the D/E edge of the C/D/E piece to complete a Spin block. Press seam toward F.

Figure 3a

4. Repeat steps 1–3 to make 16 Spin blocks.

Completing the Pieced Top

1. Arrange the Spin blocks in sets of four, coordinating the charm square areas to create a spinning flower as shown in Figure 4a.

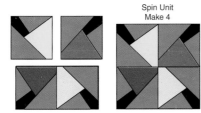

Spin Unit
Make 4

Figure 4a

2. Join two of the Spin blocks into a row. Repeat to make two rows. Join the two rows to make a Spin unit as seen in Figure 4a. Repeat to make four Spin units.

3. Carefully remove paper from each Spin unit and press.

4. Join a B triangle to opposite sides of a Spin unit (Figure 5a). Press seams toward B. Repeat to make two top/bottom rows.

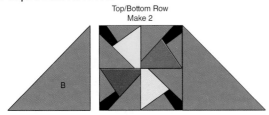

Top/Bottom Row
Make 2

Figure 5a

5. Join a Spin unit to opposite sides of A to make the center row (Figure 6a). Press seams toward A.

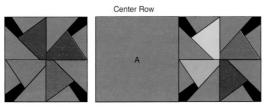

Center Row

Figure 6a

6. Refer to the Placement Diagram and sew a top/bottom row to either side of the center row to complete the pieced top.

Completing the Table Mat

1. Press the table mat top on both sides; check for proper seam pressing and trim all loose threads.

2. Sandwich batting between the stitched top and the prepared backing piece; pin or baste layers together to hold. Mark quilting design and quilt as desired by hand or machine.

3. When quilting is complete, remove pins or basting. Trim batting and backing fabric edges even with raw edges of quilt top.

4. Join binding strips on short ends with diagonal seams to make one long strip; trim seams to ¼" and press seams open.

5. Fold the binding strip in half with wrong sides together along length; press.

6. Sew binding to quilt edges, matching raw edges, mitering corners and overlapping ends.

7. Fold binding to the back side and stitch in place to finish.

8. Stack a colored ¾" button on a black 1¼" button and stitch to table mat at center of Spin units referring to Placement Diagram to finish. ∎

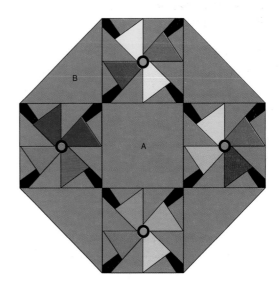

Spinning Flower Table Mat
Placement Diagram 24" x 24"

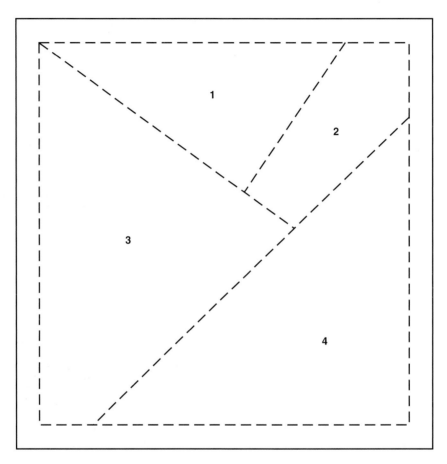

Spin Block Paper-Piecing Pattern
Refer to instructions for color placement.

Mystic Garden Bed Runner

Add a touch of spring to your bed. This will make you happy you chose charms.

Project Specifications
Skill Level: Confident Beginner
Bed Runner Size: 67½" x 24¾"
Block Size: 8" x 8"
Number of Blocks: 6

Designer Note
For this project, choose charm squares that blend well together. The sample's charm squares are a whimsical, bright floral and geometric design mix. Because the blades of the pinwheel in this design are larger pieces, you can use larger prints.

Materials
- 30 coordinating charm squares
- ¼ yard fuchsia
- ¼ yard orange
- ⅜ yard purple
- ⅝ yard green floral
- ⅔ yard green
- 2 yards blue floral
- Backing 75" x 33"
- Batting 75" x 33"
- 6 (1") buttons
- 24 sheets 8½" x 11" paper (paper piecing only)
- Fabric glue stick (paper piecing only—optional)
- Template material (alternate piecing only)
- 6 (⅞") buttons, different coordinating colors
- Neutral-color all-purpose thread
- Quilting thread
- Basic sewing tools and supplies

Cutting
1. Prepare a yo-yo template referring to Alternate Template Piecing on page 7 in the General Instructions. Choose six charm squares and use the yo-yo template on page 55 to cut six yo-yo circles. *Note: The remaining 24 charm squares do not need precutting for this paper-piecing pattern.*

2. Cut three 2" by fabric width fuchsia strips; subcut into (24) 2" x 4" paper-piecing shapes.

3. Cut three 1½" by fabric width orange B strips.

4. Cut three 3" by fabric width purple C strips.

5. Cut two 8⅞" by fabric width green floral strips; subcut five 8⅞" squares. Cut each square on one diagonal to make 10 A triangles.

6. Cut four 5" by fabric width green strips; subcut (48) 3¼" x 5" paper-piecing shapes.

7. Cut two 4½" x 56" D strips lengthwise from blue floral. *Note: Use the remainder of the blue floral for the bed runner backing.*

Paper-Piecing Instructions
Completing the Mystic Blocks

Mystic
8" x 8" Block
Make 6

1. Make 24 copies of the Spin paper-piecing pattern, referring to the General Instructions on page 5 for paper and copying choices.

2. Complete the paper piecing in numerical order as indicated on the pattern and following the General Instructions on page 6 using similar-sized fabric shapes (Figure 1). Place green shapes in areas 1 and 4, the fuchsia shape in area 2 and the charm square shape in area 3.

Make 24

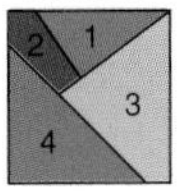

Figure 1

House of White Birches, Berne, Indiana 46711   Clotilde.com

3. Arrange the Spin units in sets of four, coordinating the charm square areas to create a spinning flower as shown in Figure 2.

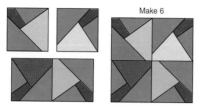

Figure 2

4. Join two of the Spinning Flower units into a row. Repeat to make two rows. Join the two rows to make a Mystic block as seen in Figure 2. Repeat to make six Mystic blocks.

5. Carefully remove paper from each Mystic block and press.

Completing the Pieced Top

1. Join an A triangle to one side of a Mystic block as seen in Figure 3 to make End A. Press seam toward A.

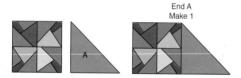

Figure 3

2. Refer to Figure 4 for positioning and join another A triangle to the opposite side of a Mystic block to make End B. Press seam toward A.

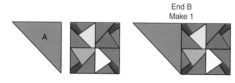

Figure 4

3. Join an A triangle to opposite sides of a Mystic block referring to Figure 5 for orientation of the A triangles. Press seams toward A. Repeat to make 4 rows.

Figure 5

4. Stitch the rows together with End A and B units as shown in Figure 6 to make pieced center. Press seams in one direction.

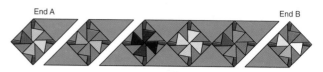

Figure 6

5. Stitch the B strips together on short ends to make one strip; press seams to one side. Cut strip in half to make two B strips.

6. Press B strips in half lengthwise wrong sides together to make two B flange strips.

7. Center and baste a B flange strip to the right side of each long edge of the pieced center, matching long raw edges (Figure 7).

Figure 7

8. Stitch the C strips together on the short ends to make one long strip pressing seams in one direction. Cut the strip in half to make two C border strips. Repeat with the D strips to make two D border strips.

9. Join C and D border strips along long edges to make two C/D borders. Press seams toward C strips.

10. Join a C/D border strip to opposite long sides of the pieced center as seen in Figure 8. Press seams toward block row.

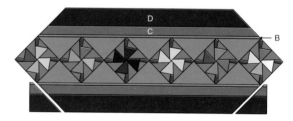

Figure 8

11. Lay a ruler along the angled end of the pieced center even with the end Spinning Flower block, again referring to Figure 8. Trim the corner of the pieced center along the ruler. Trim on all four corners.

Completing the Quilt

1. Press quilt top on both sides; check for proper seam pressing and trim all loose threads.

2. Sandwich batting between the stitched top and the prepared backing piece; pin or baste layers together to hold. Mark quilting design and quilt as desired by hand or machine.

3. When quilting is complete, remove pins or basting. Trim batting and backing fabric edges even with raw edges of quilt top.

4. Join binding strips on short ends with diagonal seams to make one long strip; trim seams to ¼" and press seams open.

5. Fold the binding strip in half with wrong sides together along length; press.

6. Sew binding to quilt edges, matching raw edges, mitering corners and overlapping ends.

7. Fold binding to the back side and stitch in place.

8. To make a yo-yo refer to Figure 9, finger-press ⅜" to the wrong side of a yo-yo circle. Hand-stitch in place around the circle taking a backstitch at the beginning to secure the thread. Gently pull the thread to tightly gather the outer edge to the center of the circle. Flatten the circle. Repeat to make six yo-yos.

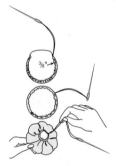

Figure 9

9. Baste a yo-yo in the center of each Spinning Flower block. Sew a ⅞" button over the center of the yo-yo through all thicknesses to complete the bed runner referring to the Placement Diagram.

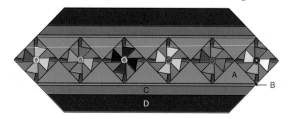

Mystic Garden Bed Runner
Placement Diagram 67½" x 24¾"

Alternate Piecing Instructions

Designer Note

The following instructions use the same materials listed for the paper-piecing instructions above. Project specifications are the same. However, cutting and construction instructions are different.

Mystic
8" x 8" Block
Make 6

Cutting

1. Prepare templates C–F on page 56 and a yo-yo referring to page 7 in the General Instructions.

2. Choose six charm squares and use the yo-yo template on page 55 to cut six yo-yo circles.

3. Use template D to cut 24 D pieces from the remaining charm squares.

4. Use template E to cut 24 fuchsia E pieces.

5. Cut three 1½" by fabric width orange G strips.

6. Cut three 3" by fabric width purple H strips.

7. Cut two 8⅞" by fabric width green floral strips; subcut five 8⅞" squares. Cut each square on one diagonal to make 10 I triangles.

8. Use templates C and F to cut 24 each green C and F pieces.

9. Cut two 4½" x 56" J strips lengthwise from blue floral. **Note:** *Use the remainder for the bed runner backing.*

Completing the Mystic Blocks

1. Refer to Figure 1a and join a C piece to an E piece; press seam toward C.

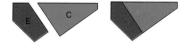

Figure 1a

2. Join D to C/E along C/E edge as shown in Figure 2a; press seam toward D.

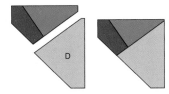

Figure 2a

3. Join F to D/E edge of C/E/D piece as shown in Figure 3a; press seam toward F to make a Spinning Flower unit.

Figure 3a

4. Repeat steps 1–3 to make 24 Spinning Flower units.

5. Arrange the Spinning Flower units in six sets of four units, coordinating the charm square areas to create a spinning flower as shown in Figure 4a.

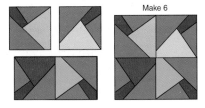

Figure 4a

6. Join two of the Spinning Flower units into a row. Repeat to make two rows. Join the two rows to make a Mystic block, referring again to Figure 4a. Repeat to make six Mystic blocks.

7. Carefully remove paper from each Mystic block and press.

Completing the Pieced Top

1. Join an I triangle to one side of a Mystic block as shown in Figure 5a to make End A. Press seam toward A.

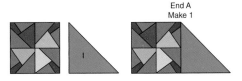

Figure 5a

2. Refer to Figure 6a for positioning and join another I triangle to the opposite side of a Mystic block to make End B. Press seam toward A.

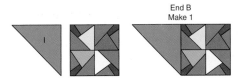

Figure 6a

3. Join an I triangle to opposite sides of a Mystic block referring to Figure 7a for orientation of the I triangles. Press seams toward I. Repeat to make 4 rows.

Figure 7a

4. Stitch the rows together with End A and B units as shown in Figure 8a to make pieced center. Press seams in one direction.

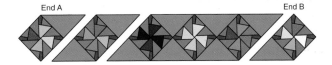

Figure 8a

5. Stitch the G strips together on short ends to make one strip; press seams to one side. Cut strip in half to make two G strips.

6. Press G strips in half lengthwise wrong sides together to make two G flange strips.

7. Center and baste a G flange strip to the right side of each long edge of the pieced center, matching raw edges (Figure 9a).

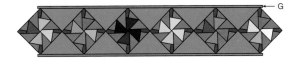

Figure 9a

8. Repeat step 5 with the H and J strips making two strips of each.

9. Join one each H and J border strips along long edges to make an H/J border. Press seams toward H strip. Repeat to make two H/J borders.

10. Center and join an H/J border strip to opposite long sides of the pieced center as shown in Figure 10a. Press seams toward block row.

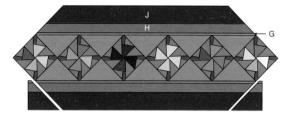

Figure 10a

11. Lay a ruler along the angled end of the pieced center even with the end Spinning Flower block, again referring to Figure 10a. Trim the corner of the pieced center along the ruler. Repeat to trim all four corners.

Completing the Quilt

1. Press quilt top on both sides; check for proper seam pressing and trim all loose threads.

2. Sandwich batting between the stitched top and the prepared backing piece; pin or baste layers together to hold. Mark quilting design and quilt as desired by hand or machine.

3. When quilting is complete, remove pins or basting. Trim batting and backing fabric edges even with raw edges of quilt top.

4. Join binding strips on short ends with diagonal seams to make one long strip; trim seams to ¼" and press seams open.

5. Fold the binding strip in half with wrong sides together along length; press.

6. Sew binding to quilt edges, matching raw edges, mitering corners and overlapping ends.

7. Fold binding to the back side and stitch in place to finish.

8. To make a yo-yo refer to Figure 11a, finger-press ⅜" to the wrong side of a yo-yo circle. Hand-stitch in place around the circle taking a backstitch at the beginning to secure the thread. Gently pull the thread to tightly gather the outer edge to the center of the circle. Flatten the circle. Repeat to make six yo-yos.

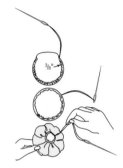

Figure 11a

9. Baste a yo-yo in the center of each Spinning Flower block. Sew a ⅞" button over the center of the yo-yo through all thicknesses to complete the bed runner referring to the Placement Diagram. ■

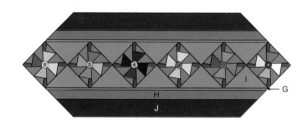

Mystic Garden Bed Runner
Placement Diagram A 67½" x 24¾"

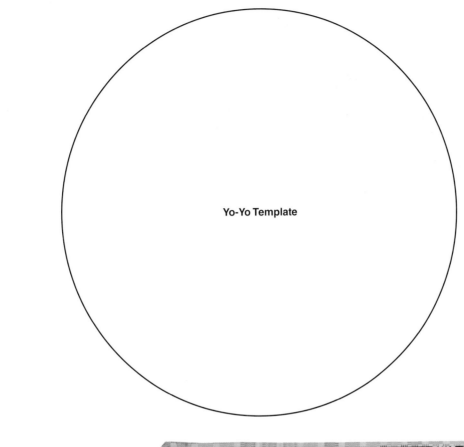

Yo-Yo Template

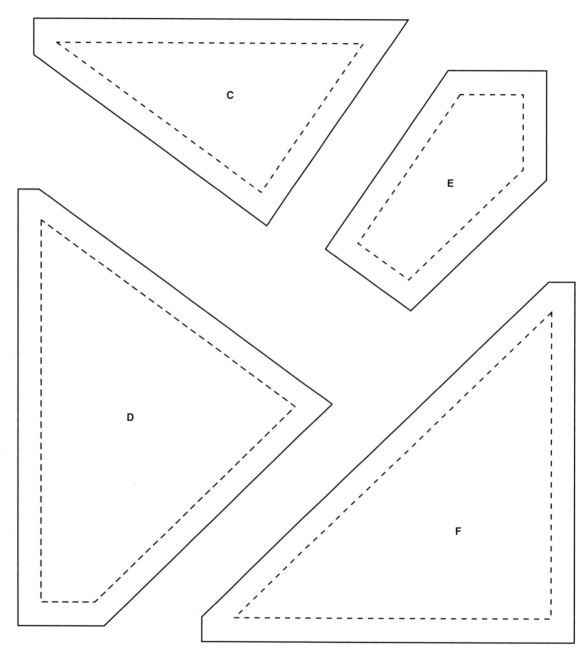

Spinning Flower Table Mat/Mystic Garden Bed Runner Alternate Piecing Templates
Cut per instructions

All Squared Up

This scrap-friendly project will use up all those leftover charms and scraps. All prints will work, and the black makes them pop!

Project Specifications
Skill Level: Beginner
Quilt Size: 57" x 67"
Block Size: 9" x 9"
Number of Blocks: 20

Squared Up
9" x 9" Block
Make 20

Designer Note
This quilt is meant to be made from leftover charms and scraps from previous projects. Cut pieces for the quilt from scraps each time you finish a project. Set them aside and when you are ready to make the quilt, you'll have a head start toward making … how many squares?

Materials
- 102 charm squares
- ½ yard white, tonal or solid
- 3 yards solid black
- Backing 65" x 75"
- Batting 65" x 75"
- Neutral-color all-purpose thread
- Quilting thread
- Basic sewing tools and supplies

Cutting
1. Cut 64 charm squares in half on one diagonal to make 128 B triangles as shown in Cutting Diagram A.

Cutting Diagram A

2. Refer to Cutting Diagram B to cut two 1½" x 4½" E rectangles and one 1½" square from each of 38 charm squares, cutting a total of 76 E rectangles and 20 D squares.

Cutting Diagram B

3. Cut (13) 1½" by fabric width white strips; subcut (80) 1½" x 4½" C and (98) 1½" F squares.

4. Cut five 2½" by fabric width black I/J strips.

5. Cut six 3½" by fabric width black L/K strips.

6. Cut seven 5" by fabric width black strips; subcut (56) 5" squares. Cut each square on one diagonal to cut a total of 112 A triangles.

7. Cut one 4½" by fabric width black strip; subcut four 2½" x 4½" H rectangles.

8. Cut the remainder of the strip into two 1½"-wide strips, subcut (31) 1½" G squares.

Completing the Blocks
1. Join A to B along long edge to make a half square (Figure 1). Press seam toward A and trim to 4½" square. Repeat to make 112 A-B half square units.

Figure 1

2. Using remaining 16 B triangles, join two different-color B triangles together along long edge to make a B-B half square unit (Figure 2). Press seam toward darker color and trim to 4½". Repeat to make eight B-B half square units.

Figure 2

3. Join the B edges of two different A-B units to opposite long sides of C referring to Figure 3 to make a block row. Press seams toward A-B. Repeat to make 40 block rows. ***Note:*** *Do not put the same color A-B units in one row.*

Make 40

Figure 3

4. Join two C strips to opposite sides of D (Figure 4). Press seams toward D. Repeat to make 20 C-D center block rows.

Make 20

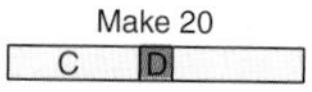

Figure 4

5. Join a block row to opposite sides of a center block row making sure the B/C edges of the rows are next to the center block row, refer to Figure 5 for orientation. ***Note:*** *Do not put the same colors together in one block.*

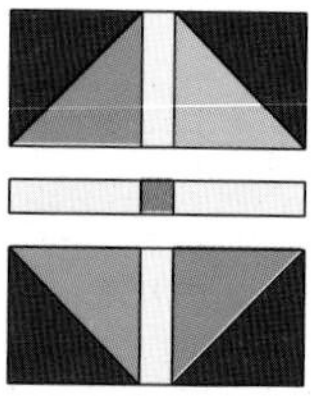

Figure 5

6. Repeat step 5 to make 20 Squared Up blocks, referring to block diagram.

Completing the Pieced Center

1. Choose eight different E strips, four G squares and three F squares. Refer to Figure 6 and join the E strips alternately with the G and F squares to make a sashing row. Repeat to make four sashing rows.

Make 4

Figure 6

2. Join two different E strips to opposite sides of G (Figure 7). Press seams toward G. Repeat to make 15 sashing strips.

Make 15

Figure 7

3. To make a row, join four blocks alternately with sashing strips, beginning and ending with a block as shown in Figure 8. Press seams toward blocks. Repeat to make five rows.

Make 5
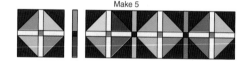

Figure 8

4. Stitch five rows and four sashing rows together alternately, beginning with a block row as shown in Figure 9. Press seams in one direction to complete the pieced center.

Figure 9

60

Completing the Pieced Borders

1. Choose eight A-B units, two B-B units, four C, three E and two H. Refer to Figure 10 and join pieces in order shown, alternating C and E; press seams away from A-B and B-B units. Repeat to make two top/bottom pieced borders.

Figure 10

2. Choose eight A-B units, two B-B units, five C and four E. Refer to Figure 11 and join pieces in order shown alternating C and E; press seams away from A-B and B-B units. Repeat to make two side pieced borders.

Figure 11

3. Stitch I/J strips together on short ends; press seams in one direction. Cut two 49½" I border strips and two 51½" J border strips.

4. Repeat step 3 with the L/K strips. Cut two 57½" L border strips and two 62½" K border strips.

5. Stitch an I border strip to the black side of the A-B units in the top/bottom pieced border referring to Figure 12. Repeat to make two top/bottom pieced borders.

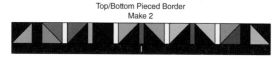

Figure 12

6. Repeat step 5 with J border strips and side pieced borders to make two side pieced borders as shown in Figure 13.

Figure 13

Completing the Quilt

1. Stitch side pieced borders to opposite sides of the pieced center with the side pieced borders J side next to the pieced center (Figure 14).

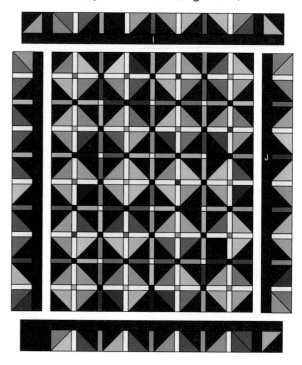

Figure 14

2. Repeat step 1 stitching the top/bottom pieced borders to the pieced center with the I side of the pieced borders next to the pieced center, again referring to Figure 14.

3. Stitch the K border strips to opposite sides of the quilt and L border strips to the top and bottom of the quilt referring to the Placement Diagram.

4. Press quilt top on both sides; check for proper seam pressing and trim all loose threads.

5. Sandwich batting between the stitched top and the prepared backing piece; pin or baste layers together to hold. Mark quilting design and quilt as desired by hand or machine.

6. When quilting is complete, remove pins or basting. Trim batting and backing fabric edges even with raw edges of quilt top.

7. Join binding strips on short ends with diagonal seams to make one long strip; trim seams to ¼" and press seams open.

8. Fold the binding strip in half with wrong sides together along length; press.

9. Sew binding to quilt edges, matching raw edges, mitering corners and overlapping ends.

10. Fold binding to the back side and stitch in place to finish. ■

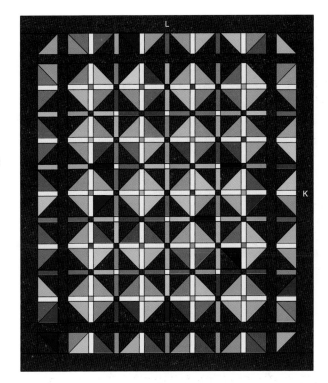

All Squared Up
Placement Diagram 57" x 67"

House of White Birches, Berne, Indiana 46711   Clotilde.com

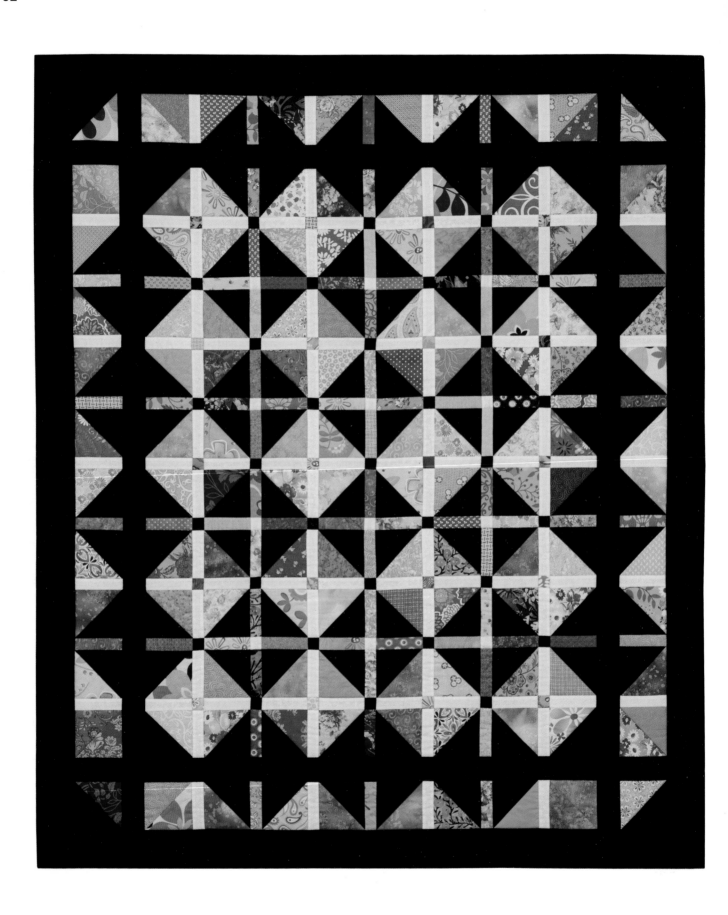

METRIC CONVERSION CHARTS

Metric Conversions

Canada/U.S. Measurement		Multiplied by		Metric Measurement
yards	x	.9144	=	metres (m)
yards	x	91.44	=	centimetres (cm)
inches	x	2.54	=	centimetres (cm)
inches	x	25.40	=	millimetres (mm)
inches	x	.0254	=	metres (m)

Canada/U.S. Measurement		Multiplied by		Metric Measurement
centimetres	x	.3937	=	inches
metres	x	1.0936	=	yards

Standard Equivalents

Canada/U.S. Measurement		Metric Measurement		
⅛ inch	=	3.20 mm	=	0.32 cm
¼ inch	=	6.35 mm	=	0.635 cm
⅜ inch	=	9.50 mm	=	0.95 cm
½ inch	=	12.70 mm	=	1.27 cm
⅝ inch	=	15.90 mm	=	1.59 cm
¾ inch	=	19.10 mm	=	1.91 cm
⅞ inch	=	22.20 mm	=	2.22 cm
1 inches	=	25.40 mm	=	2.54 cm
⅛ yard	=	11.43 cm	=	0.11 m
¼ yard	=	22.86 cm	=	0.23 m
⅜ yard	=	34.29 cm	=	0.34 m
½ yard	=	45.72 cm	=	0.46 m
⅝ yard	=	57.15 cm	=	0.57 m
¾ yard	=	68.58 cm	=	0.69 m
⅞ yard	=	80.00 cm	=	0.80 m
1 yard	=	91.44 cm	=	0.91 m
1⅛ yards	=	102.87 cm	=	1.03 m
1¼ yards	=	114.30 cm	=	1.14 m

Canada/U.S. Measurement		Metric Measurement		
1⅜ yards	=	125.73 cm	=	1.26 m
1½ yards	=	137.16 cm	=	1.37 m
1⅝ yards	=	148.59 cm	=	1.49 m
1¾ yards	=	160.02 cm	=	1.60 m
1⅞ yards	=	171.44 cm	=	1.71 m
2 yards	=	182.88 cm	=	1.83 m
2⅛ yards	=	194.31 cm	=	1.94 m
2¼ yards	=	205.74 cm	=	2.06 m
2⅜ yards	=	217.17 cm	=	2.17 m
2½ yards	=	228.60 cm	=	2.29 m
2⅝ yards	=	240.03 cm	=	2.40 m
2¾ yards	=	251.46 cm	=	2.51 m
2⅞ yards	=	262.88 cm	=	2.63 m
3 yards	=	274.32 cm	=	2.74 m
3⅛ yards	=	285.75 cm	=	2.86 m
3¼ yards	=	297.18 cm	=	2.97 m
3⅜ yards	=	308.61 cm	=	3.09 m
3½ yards	=	320.04 cm	=	3.20 m
3⅝ yards	=	331.47 cm	=	3.31 m
3¾ yards	=	342.90 cm	=	3.43 m
3⅞ yards	=	354.32 cm	=	3.54 m
4 yards	=	365.76 cm	=	3.66 m
4⅛ yards	=	377.19 cm	=	3.77 m
4¼ yards	=	388.62 cm	=	3.89 m
4⅜ yards	=	400.05 cm	=	4.00 m
4½ yards	=	411.48 cm	=	4.11 m
4⅝ yards	=	422.91 cm	=	4.23 m
4¾ yards	=	434.34 cm	=	4.34 m
4⅞ yards	=	445.76 cm	=	4.46 m
5 yards	=	457.20 cm	=	4.57 m

HOUSE of
WHITE
BIRCHES
PUBLISHERS
SINCE 1947

ISBN: 978-1-59217-374-7

1 2 3 4 5 6 7 8 9

Photo Index

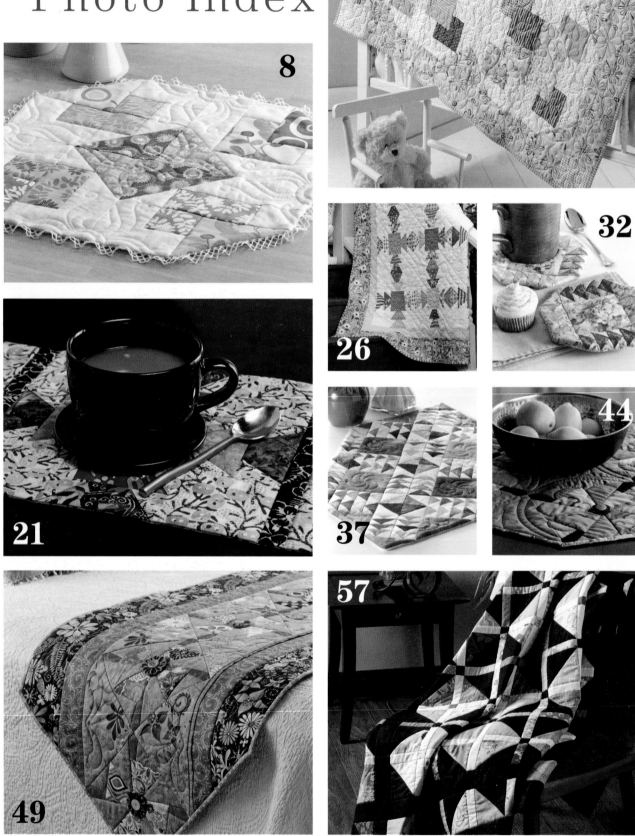

8

16

21

26

32

37

44

49

57